D0387037

Moments
for
Pastors

Moments

for

Pastors

by
Robert Strand

New Leaf Press

First printing, March 1995
Second printing, February 1997

ISBN: 0-89221-289-6
Library of Congress: 94-73973

Interior photos by D. Jeanene Tiner, House Springs, Missouri

All Scripture references are from the New International Version, unless
otherwise noted.

Every effort has been made to locate the authors or originators of the
stories contained in this book. Most are the result of conversations with
pastors, while others were accumulated throughout the course of a 30-year
radio and television broadcasting career.

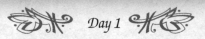

Praying Hands

The famous "Praying Hands" picture was created by Albrecht Durer, the son of a Hungarian goldsmith. He was born in Germany in 1471 and died in 1528. As is the case with nearly all men of genius, fact and fiction become interwoven and created the legend of the artist as we know him today.

It is said, that while studying art, Albert, as he was called, and a friend roomed together. However, the meager income they earned on the side as they studied did not prove to be enough to meet their needs for rent, food, clothing, and other living expenses. Albert suggested that he would go to work to earn the necessary income for both of them while his friend pursued and finished his art studies. When finished, the friend would then go to work to provide support while Durer would finish his studies. The friend was pleased and happy with the plan, except that he insisted that he be the first to work and that Albert continue his studies.

This plan was followed and in time Albert Durer became a skilled artist and engraver. Returning to his room one day, Albert announced that he was now ready to assume the burden of support, while his friend studied art. But, as a result of his hard labor, his friend's hands were so swollen that he was no longer able to hold and use the paintbrush with skill. His career as an artist was ended.

Albert was deeply saddened by this disappointment which his friend had suffered. One day when he returned to their room he heard his friend praying and saw his hands held in a reverent attitude of prayer. At this moment, Albert received the inspiration to create the picture of those wonderful "praying hands." His friend's lost skill could never be restored but in and through this picture, Durer felt that he could express his love and appreciation for the self-sacrificing labor which his friend had performed for him. Durer also had another thought that such a picture could inspire a like appreciation on the part of others who may also be willing to sacrifice and give on the behalf of someone else.

The story is now legend. I cannot verify if this is factual or not, but it sounds wonderful. Self-sacrificing is a brand of love that is not too often seen in our too-busy kind of a world. Yes, in the act of sacrificial love we have identity as being part of the body of Jesus Christ, otherwise known as the Church. Humble giving and prayer are keys to open Heaven's door.

Today's Quote: *I long to accomplish a great and noble task, but it is my chief duty and joy to accomplish humble tasks as though they were great and noble . . . for the world is moved along, not only by the mighty shoves of its heroes, but also by the aggregate of tiny pushes of each honest worker!* — Helen Keller

Today's Verse: By this all will know that you are My disciples, if you have love for one another (John 13:35;NKJ).

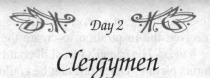

Clergymen

A country preacher was preaching very pointedly to his congregation one Sunday morning.

He said, "Now let the church walk!"

Deacon Jones said, "AMEN, let it walk!"

The preacher then said, "Let the church run!"

Deacon Jones said, "AMEN, Parson, let it run!"

"Let the church fly!" shouted the preacher.

"AMEN, brother, let it fly!" shouted Deacon Jones.

"Now it's going to take a lot of money to let it fly, brother," shouted the preacher.

"Let it walk, then," said Deacon Jones, "let it walk."

Preachers can be funny people. I'm one myself, and know quite a few other preachers. Most have discovered that it helps to develop a sense of humor. Many times we are caught in situations when nothing works. It's at such times that it helps to laugh at the situation and at ourselves.

There was a small town preacher who rushed to the railroad station every afternoon to watch the 3:08 train go by. Members of his congregation thought his pastime was too juvenile and so his church board asked him to give it up.

"No, gentlemen," he said firmly. "I preach your sermons, teach your Sunday school, bury your dead, marry your young people, run your charities, and am chairman of every drive it pleases you to conduct. I pray at every function you have. I won't give it up, this seeing the train every day. I love it! It's the only think that passes through this town that I don't have to organize or push or pull!"

And there was a young, rookie preacher who was quite flattered when someone described him as a "model" preacher.

His pride soon vanished when he turned to his dictionary and found the definition of "model:" A small imitation of the real thing.

He used a bit more caution the next time. On being described as a "warm" preacher, he turned to his pocket dictionary which read: "Warm . . . not so hot."

The next time you see your pastor, how about praying for him? In fact, how about doing it now? No one in your community sees as thin a slice of life as your local preacher. He needs your support as well as your presence in church.

Today's Quote: *I preached as never sure to preach again, and as a dying man to dying men!* — Richard Baxter

Today's Verse: It was He who "gave gifts to men;" He appointed some to be apostles, others to be prophets, others to be evangelists, others to be pastors and teachers (Eph. 4:11;TEV).

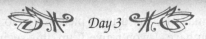

Shocking Generosity

The story goes that while Robert Smith was taking his afternoon walk as part of his therapy in recovering from a massive heart attack, the phone rang and his wife Delores answered. The call was from the Reader's Digest Association Sweepstakes in New York. They were calling to inform the Smith family that Robert had just won $1,500,000 and that in a few days the certified check would be arriving. Well, as you can imagine, Delores was absolutely ecstatic. Now all those dreams would come true!

But then she remembered, her husband was just getting over his massive heart attack and the doctor had said no excitement over anything. Delores was afraid that if she told him they had just won such a large sum, he would have another heart attack and die. What should she do? After some thought, she decided to call their pastor and ask his advice because he had had some experience in breaking difficult news to families.

Delores dialed, "Hello, Pastor Baldwin . . . this is Delores Smith."

The pastor replied, "Hi, Delores. How are you? And how is Bob?"

"I'm fine, thank you. And so is Bob. He's recovering nicely. But, I've got a problem and I need your advice."

"Sure, if I can help, I'll be glad to," the pastor replied.

"Well, Pastor, I just got a call from The Reader's Digest Sweepstakes informing me that Bob has just won $1,500,000!"

"That's great!" said the pastor, "But what's the problem?"

"Well, I'm afraid that if I tell Bob, he'll get so excited that he will have another heart attack and drop dead. Can you help me?"

"Well, Delores, I think I can. Hold on, I'll be right over."

So in about an hour, Bob is now back from his walk and he and Delores and Pastor Baldwin are in the den having a nice chat. The pastor leans toward Bob and says, "Bob, I've got a problem and need your advice."

"Sure, Pastor, if I can help, I'll be glad to," Bob said.

The pastor takes a deep breath and goes on, "It's a theoretical situation regarding Christian stewardship. What would a person — take you for instance — do if all of a sudden you found out you had won $1,500,000? What would you do with all that money?"

"That's easy," Bill replied, "I'd start by giving $750,000 to the church."

Whereupon, Pastor Baldwin had a heart attack and dropped dead!

Today's Quote: *We make a living by what we get out of life but we make a life by what we give!* — Doyal Van Gelder

Today's Verse: Give, and there will be gifts for you: a full measure, pressed down, shaken together, and running over, will be poured into your lap; because the amount you measure out is the amount you will be given back (Luke 6:38;JB).

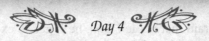

The Dignity of the Robe

A seminary president tells this story: In our particular denomination, when candidates are ordained into the ministry, they each have one thing assigned to them to do in that particular ordination service. The services are solemn, dignified, impressive, and meaningful.

At the conclusion of the worship/ordination service this candidate was to stand, walk up the steps into the chancel, turn, and pronounce the benediction. This was to be his very first official act as a newly ordained minister.

The time arrived, the candidate solemnly stood, approached the steps, and ascended. But on the first step, he stepped inside the hem of his clerical robe. This poor candidate/ordainee kept climbing up the steps . . . all the time walking up the inside of his robe. Each step made him smaller as he was forced to "duck walk" up the inside of his own robe.

Finally, at the top of the steps, looking like some kind of a dwarf in a white tent, he turned around. His robe could not turn with him, since he was standing inside it. The act of turning placed the left arm of his robe right in the center of his chest and the right arm was somewhere between his shoulders. All he could move was his left wrist from the center of his chest, arms pressed tight against his body by the constriction of the robe. With a wave of his wrist he pronounced the benediction, solemnly, not missing a word.

When he was finished, unable to take another step from his duck walk posture inside his robe, he was helpless. Two husky ushers came forward, picked him up by his armpits and carried him off like some piece of furniture.[1]

I wish I could have been there! How about you?

Ministry is so wonderful . . . the humor is explosive and subtle and so unexpected!

Do you ever think what might have happened to the Sermon on the Mount if Jesus had to speak through a sound system? Use a tape system that didn't tape? A faulty organ with a late organist? Use word processors that don't process? It's amazing that the Church still marches on in spite of technology and what we do to it ourselves. Oh, well!

Today's Quote: *A sense of humor . . . is not so much the ability to appreciate humorous stories as it is . . . the capacity to recognize the absurdity of the positions one gets into from time to time together with skill in retreating from them with dignity.* — Dana L. Farnsworth

Today's Verse: Then he said to them, "Go your way, eat the fat, drink the sweet, and send portions to those for whom nothing is prepared; for this day is holy to our Lord. Do not sorrow, for the joy of the Lord is your strength" (Neh. 8:10;NKJV).

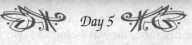

Part of the Gift

A missionary was sent to Africa to be part of a ministry already in the works. This man had been raised on the Pacific Coast of the United States and loved the ocean. He had hoped that when sent to Africa he would be stationed in an area next to the ocean. His wish was not fulfilled, and upon his arrival he found his mission station was about 85 miles inland from the coast.

He determined to make the best of his assignment. Part of his responsibilities involved teaching in a Bible school in the area. It had been set up to provide ministerial training for the natives so that they could be effective evangelists to their own people.

In his teaching, many times this missionary-teacher would draw upon the ocean for his illustrative material. Often he talked of his great love for the ocean which he missed being this far inland. His students made note of his affection for the sea.

In the course of his teaching he began to teach about the fact that much of the Christian life is one of giving. He spoke about Christ being given as a special gift to this earth when He came as a babe in a manger. He shared with the native students about Christmas. He wasn't at all sure that the concept had been picked up, but he did the best he knew how about giving.

Then there was time for a break in the school year as the students were dismissed for a two-week period.

One day during this break there was a knock on his door. The missionary went to the door to see one of his students standing there with a huge smile on his face. Upon taken a closer look he noticed that the young man had scratches on his face, arms, and legs. His clothes looked like he had been on a long trek through jungle and formidable terrain. There was a tiredness about the young man.

However, in his hands this black man was holding a basketful of sea shells. Obviously they were not to be found locally. Then it dawned on the missionary — this young man had walked to the ocean to bring them back.

"Here is a gift from the ocean," the young man beamed.

The missionary was almost overcome with emotion as he replied, "But you have walked almost 170 miles to do this!"

His black face showed surprise and delight. He pulled himself to his full height and said, "Long walk is part of the gift!"

Today's Quote: *The greatest grace is a gift, perhaps, in that it anticipates no return!* — Longfellow

Today's Verse: But just as you excel in everything — in faith, in speech, in knowledge, in complete earnestness and in your love for us — see that you also excel in this grace of giving (2 Cor. 8:7).

Sifting

A "house-church" in a city of the USSR had managed to receive a single copy of the Gospel according to Luke. This was the only written copy of the Scripture that many of these Christians had ever seen. They tore it into small sections and distributed them among this body of believers. Their plan was to memorize the portion they had been given, then on the next Sunday they would meet and redistribute the scriptural sections to memorize more.

On Sunday, these believers arrived inconspicuously in small groups or as singles throughout the day so as not to arouse the suspicion of KGB informers. By dark they were all safely inside, windows closed and doors were locked. They began by singing a hymn quietly but with deep emotion.

Suddenly, the door was forced open and in walked two soldiers with loaded automatic weapons. One shouted, "All right, everyone line up against the wall. If you wish to renounce your commitment to Jesus Christ, leave now!"

Two or three quickly left, then another. After a few moments, two more.

"This is your last chance. Either turn against your faith in Christ," he ordered, "or stay and suffer the consequences."

Another left. Finally, two more in embarrassed silence with their faces covered, slipped out into the night. No one else moved. Parents with small children trembling beside them, looked down reassuringly. They fully expected to be gunned down or at best, to be imprisoned.

After a few more moments of complete silence, the other soldier closed the door, looked back at those who stood against the wall and said, "Keep your hands up . . . but this time in praise to our Lord Jesus Christ. Brothers and sisters, we, too, are Christians! We were sent to another house church several weeks ago to arrest a group of believers."

The other soldier interrupted, "But, instead, we were converted! We have learned by experience, however, that unless people are willing to die for their faith, they cannot be fully trusted."

Stories like this from the underground church in Russia have a way of jolting us! Immediately, this question comes to my mind: Would I be willing to die for my faith in Jesus Christ? Talk about a commitment. Yet, it was exactly this kind of total giving that brought our modern day church into being. Pioneers have gone before who were willing to give everything, including life to preserve and spread this gospel! Can we do less?

Today's Quote: *Real convictions disturb. They also attract!* — Eleanor Doan

Today's Verse: Commit thy way unto the Lord; trust also in Him; and He shall bring it to pass (Ps. 37:5;KJV).

It Makes a Difference

It was early in 1945. As United States forces pushed deep into Okinawa they came across a village unlike any they had ever seen. Here at Shimabuku they were met and welcomed by two old men who invited the troops in as "fellow Christians."

Correspondent Clarence W. Hall described the hamlet like this: "We'd seen other Okinawan villages, uniformly down at the heels and despairing; by contrast this one shone like a diamond in a dung heap. Everywhere we were greeted by smiles and dignified bows. Proudly the old men showed us their spotless homes, their terraced fields, fertile and neat, their storehouses and granaries, and their prized sugar mill."

Searching for an answer as to why this one village was so different from all the rest, Hall uncovered an incredible story. Some 30 years before, an American missionary on his way to Japan had paused at Ahimabuku and stayed only long enough to make two converts and leave them a Japanese translated Bible. These new converts, with only instructions to read the Bible and live by it, began sharing their faith with neighbors. Before long the whole town had accepted Christ and for 30 years had been following the Bible completely.

They had adopted the Ten Commandments as their legal code, the Sermon on the Mount as their guide in social conduct. In their schools they taught the Bible, and in their courts made decisions on what God's Word said.

Hall noted that they managed to create a Christian democracy at its purest. The result was that there were no jails, no bars, no drunkenness, no divorce, and a high level of happiness!

The young war correspondent was so moved by the experience that he later requisitioned a jeep and investigated this town more fully. He attended a primitive but deeply spiritual worship service and came away more impressed.

After the war came to an end, Hall began to wonder what had happened to the tiny hamlet. Fifteen years later he went back there to find that while modern civilization had swallowed Okinawa, the spiritual influence of Shimabuku remained.

On leaving the town many years before, his jeep driver had said, "So this is what comes out of only a Bible and a couple of old guys who wanted to live like Jesus." Then with a glance at a shell hole, Hall recalled the driver murmuring, "Maybe we're using the wrong weapons to make this world over!"

Today's Quote: *We can build a better world with these better weapons!*

Today's Verse: And He said unto them, Go ye into all the world, and preach the gospel to every creature (Mark 16:15;KJV).

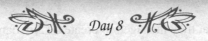

Fifty-seven Pennies

She was just a little girl, one of those non-persons. Nothing to make her stand out from other little girls. She was not from a wealthy family in fact she was from a poor family. Fifty-seven pennies were found under her pillow the night she died and this simple act made an indelible mark on the city of Philadelphia, Pennsylvania.

This little girl had made an attempt to become part of a Sunday school in Philadelphia years ago and was told she could not come because there was no room for her. She began saving her pennies in order to "help the Sunday school have more room."

Two years later she became sick and in a couple of weeks, died. Beneath her pillow they found a small, tattered book with the 57 pennies and a piece of paper on which she had printed neatly: "To help build the Little Temple bigger, so more children can go to Sunday school."

This little story and the purse with the 57 pennies were brought to the pastor, and if I have my memory on correctly, this was the Rev. Russell H. Conwell, and he told this humble story to his congregation. Then, the newspapers picked up the story and took it across the country. This triggered a spontaneous wave of gifts and giving. Soon the pennies grew and grew and today the final outcome of the humble 57 pennies offering can still be seen in Philadelphia today.

The "Little Temple" church had been replaced by a church which seats 3,300 people with lots of room for Sunday school. There is also a "Temple University" which accommodates and educates thousands of students. And there is also a "Temple Hospital" dedicated to humanity. And it all began with a nameless little girl who set out to do something about a need. Her beautiful, unselfish, dedicated attitude is what started this project. All it really takes in life to begin making a difference is one person with concern and dedication followed by an action. Let's add one more ingredient to this mix and call it love. Little people, in fact, all people are important to the future of the kingdom of God. Don't be discouraged with your little contribution. God can take your action and turn it into something big for His kingdom. Don't give up! I think of the little boy and his simple lunch . . . but in the Master's hands it was about to feed thousands and there was some left over. God needs a willing person first and watch it happen, again!

Today's Quote: *He who can give to this city better streets and better sidewalks, better schools and more colleges, more happiness, and more civilization, more of God, he will be great anywhere!* — Russell H. Conwell

Today's Verse: But Jesus called the children to him, and said, "Let the children come to me, and do not stop them, because the Kingdom of God belongs to such as these (Luke 18:16;TEV).

I Saved Nobody but Myself

Many years ago, a 25-year-old nephew of Dr. Gansaulus, a famous Chicago preacher, admitted his distress because he could find no purpose for his life. His uncle talked with him of the need to give himself for others as a means whereby such purpose could be found.

As he left the office the young man noted that the old Iroquois Theatre was burning. He saw several people trapped in an upper-story window. Quickly he found a plank, climbed to a level in the next building where he placed the plank across the window and helped several to safety. Unfortunately, a falling beam struck him and knocked him to the pavement far below. Dr. Gansaulus was called and arrived just before his nephew died. The young man looked squarely into his uncle's eyes and whispered, "Now I know why I was born."

Several years later Dr. Gansaulus was talking with another traveler in a hotel in Europe. A casual remark about Chicago so excited this man that he babbled unintelligibly; whereupon his companion led him away, explaining later to the minister that the man had been in the old Iroquois Theatre in Chicago on the fateful day it burned. He had managed to get out only by crawling and clawing his way over many screaming, fear-crazed, panic-stricken people. Ever since, at the slightest reference to Chicago, he would tremble and mutter, "I saved nobody but myself. I saved nobody but myself."[2]

The fire we're talking about happened in 1903 when Eddie Foy was there in a huge extravaganza. The place was packed with people. Fire broke out and seemed to explode as it filled and enveloped the building. Panic struck immediately! People jammed the aisles in a desperate struggle to get to the doors. Hot gases and smoke filled the place, turning it into a death chamber. A total of 590 people died. It was an awful scene.

Mainly because of this fire, public buildings were required to clearly mark their exits and install panic bars on doors that always swung outward. Fire-retardant materials were encouraged from that time as well.

There is an analogy here. One of these days this world and world system will be under the judgment of fire according to the Bible. The only place of real safety is in Jesus Christ. As Christians we have found a place of refuge and safety, but how many of our friends still need our help to lead them to Christ? Life must be lived with an eye toward eternity.

Today's Quote: *Christ's grave was the birthplace of an indestructible belief that death is vanquished and there is life eternal!* — Adolph Harnack

Today's Verse: For anyone who wants to save his life will lose it; but anyone who loses his life for my sake will find it (Matt. 16:25; JB).

The Latest Fads

A church gave its pastor a citizen's band radio for a birthday present. A month or two later he received this letter from his church board:

"Dear Pastor: We might suggest that you are getting a little carried away with your CB hobby. Last Sunday your prayer started: 'Do you read me, Big Daddy?' You then went on to describe our crowd as 'wall-to-wall and treetop-tall'.

"It was a bit much when you kept referring to Moses the Lawgiver as the 'Sinai Bear.' We believe our congregation would have better understood your sermon on the hereafter without constant reference to 'negatory purgatory.' And last, we prefer a reverential 'Amen' to 'From Holy Roller to Big Daddy . . . ten-four!' Signed, Your Church Board."

Funny, isn't it, how our language took a turn with the coming of the ever-present CB? All of us had to have a CB in our car or pickup so we could keep up with the 18 wheelers. For a time it even affected the writing of country music. It really has turned out to be another passing fad.

Our nation moves from one fad to another. If you are old enough, you can remember the Davy Crockett craze, or the hula hoop, which was really a lot of hoop-ala over nothing. Today it's designer jeans at a very inflated price.

One of the newer problems facing doctors is the "electronic wrist" which is a severe pain in the wrist from playing too many video games non-stop. It's sort of like having "tennis elbow" or a "football knee."

Where will it all stop? When will the next new wave of mania flow over us? What will be the next craze and who is the instant millionaire?

In such a changing world, is there anything that stays the same? Do we have anything on which to anchor a life? The songwriter gives us a clue:

> "On Christ the solid rock I stand,
> All other ground is sinking sand."

There is something that never changes! The methods by which the message of Jesus Christ is communicated have changed but the message and the Man are still the same yesterday, today, and forever! There is a foundation upon which you can build a life! This is not a fad that will be here today only to be discarded tomorrow. That foundation is Jesus Christ and He has an invitation for days like today: "Come to me, all you who are weary and burdened, and I will give you rest" (Matt. 11:28). Put something functional into your life.

Today's Quote: *Christ is the great central fact in the world's history; to Him everything looks forward or backward!* — Charles Hadden Spurgeon

Today's Verse: Heaven and earth shall pass away: but my words shall not pass away (Luke 21:33;KJV).

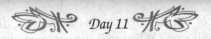

Incarnation

In 1873 a Belgian Catholic priest named Joseph Damien de Veuster was sent to minister to lepers on the Hawaiian Island of Molokai. When he arrived he immediately began to meet each of the lepers in the colony in hopes of building a friendship and a ministry. Wherever he turned, people shunned him. It seemed as though every door to ministry was closed. He poured his life into his work, erecting a chapel and beginning worship services and pouring out his heart to the lepers. But it was to no avail! No one responded to his ministry. After 12 years of rejection and failure Father Damien decided to leave.

Dejected, he made his way to the docks to board a ship to take him back home to Belgium. As he stood on the dock he wrung his hands nervously as he recounted his futile ministry among lepers. As he did he looked down at his hands . . . he noticed some mysterious white spots and felt some numbness. Almost immediately he knew what was happening to his body. He had contacted leprosy! He was now a leper!

It was at that moment he knew what he had to do. He returned to the leper colony and to his work. Quickly the word spread about his disease through the colony. Within a matter of hours everyone knew. Hundreds of them gathered outside his hut. They understood his pain, fear, and uncertainty about the future.

But the biggest surprise was the following Sunday as Father Damien arrived at the chapel to conduct the morning service. He found hundreds of worshippers already there. By the time the service began there was standing room only — the place was packed with people and many more were gathered outside the chapel!

The rest is history! Father Damien had a ministry that became enormously successful. If you have traveled to Hawaii lately, it's not long before you are reminded about that ministry. What was the reason? It's a simple concept of working with human beings . . . he was now one of them, he understood them, he hurt with them, and was able to empathize with them. There was now an identity. There was no question if he cared or not.

And this is the essence of why Christ came. There's a big word that describes this action, it's called "incarnation." It's when God became a man, a human being just like all of us.

Today's Quote: *The mystery of the humanity of Christ, that He sunk himself into our flesh, is beyond all human understanding!* — Martin Luther

Today's Verse: Teord became flesh and made his dwelling among us. We have seen the glory, the glory of the One and Only, who came from the Father, full of grace and truth (John 1:14).

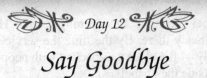

Say Goodbye

There was an old man on the isle of Crete and during his lifetime he loved many things. He loved his wife, his children, and his job, but most of all he loved the land. He loved the very ground he walked on, worked, and fought for. When it was time for him to die he had his sons bring him outside his stone cottage and lay him on the hard earth. He reached down, grabbed a handful of Crete's soil and was gone.

He arrived at the gates of heaven and the Lord came out dressed in the long robes of a judge and said to him, "Old man, come in."

As the old man moved towards the gates the Lord noticed something in his hand and said, "What are you clutching in your hand?"

He said, "It is Crete. I go nowhere without it."

The Lord said, "Leave it, or you will not be allowed in."

The old man held his clenched fist up and said, "Never!" And he went and sat beside the outside wall of the heavenly city.

After a week had passed, the gates opened again and the Lord appeared a second time, in the guise of a man wearing a hat, looking like some of the old man's buddies down in Crete. He sat down next to the old man, threw His arm around his shoulder and said, "My friend, dust belongs in the wind. Drop that piece of earth and come inside."

But the old man was still adamant. He said, "Never!"

During the third week the old man looked down at the earth he was clutching and saw that it had begun to cake and crumble. All of the moisture of the earth had gone out of it. Also, his fingers were arthritic and could not handle it. The earth began to trickle through his fingers.

Out came the Lord, this time as a small child. He came up to the old man and sat next to him and said, "Grandfather, the gates only open for those with open hands."

The old man thought about this, finally stood up, and did not even look as his hand opened and the crumbled dirt of Crete fell through the sky. The child took his hand and led him toward the glorious gates, and as the gates swung open he walked in. Inside was all of Crete.

Now don't build a theology on this story for that is what it is — a story that illustrates a point that many of us must be reminded of now and then. There is nothing here that is worth missing heaven in order to keep.

Today's Quote: *Many people hope to be elected to heaven who are not even running for the office!* — Author unknown

Today's Verse: And God shall wipe away all tears from their eyes; and there shall be no more death, neither sorrow, nor crying, neither shall there be any more pain: for the former things are passed away (Rev. 21:4;KJV).

A Second Opinion

A tourist, for the first time in his life, had carefully planned a vacation trip to the Grand Canyon. Finally the time arrived, they packed the car, and the family took off. It was the culmination of a dream vacation they had wished for, and now it was a reality. On the way they discussed what they would do, the sights they would see, and the fun they would have at the Grand Canyon. This was the father's dream. He told his family about how he would like nothing more than to walk some of the rim and take pictures looking right into the canyon itself.

Finally they arrived and checked in to a local motel, and rushed out to the canyon to begin their vacation. The first thing the father did was to make his way along the rim, but he lost his footing and plunged over the side, clawing and clutching frantically to save himself.

After he fell out of sight and just before he fell into space, he en-countered a shrubby type of bush which he desperately grabbed with both hands. Now he was hanging in mid-air, feet and body dangling over the edge, with nothing beneath him. He looked down to see the canyon floor hundreds of feet below. He was filled with terror! What would he do now? His family had been left behind at the lookout, and were too far away to hear his cry for help. Talk about a tough situation!

Filled with fear, he looked up and called out towards the empty heavens, "Is there anyone up there?"

A calm, powerful voice came out of the sky, "Yes, there is."

The tourist, feeling just a bit better since he had received an answer, pleaded, "Can you help me? Please, can you help me?"

The calm voice replied, "Yes, I probably can. What is your problem?"

"I fell over this cliff and am dangling in space holding on to a bush that is about to let go. Please help me," he again pleaded.

The voice from above said, "I'll try. Do you believe?"

"Yes, yes, I believe!"

"Do you have faith?"

"Yes, YES. I have a very strong faith!"

The calm voice said, "Well, in that case, simply let loose of the bush and everything will turn out fine."

There was a pause, then he yelled, "Is there anyone else up there?"

Today's Quote: *Faith is not faith until or unless it is translated into an action!* —Unknown

Today's Verse: What does it profit, my brethren, if someone says he has faith but does not have works? Can faith save him? (James 2:14;NKJV).

Epitaphs

Pastors spend quite a bit of their time in cemeteries . . . so if they must be there, one good diversion is to read some of the tombstones. Here are a few that have been collected by pastors from cemeteries across the country:

Here lies Lester Moore, Four slugs from a 44, No less, no more.

Seen on the grave marker of a dentist:

Stranger! Approach this spot with gravity.

John Brownis filling his last cavity.

Taken from the grave of an editor:

Here lies an editor! Snooks if you will;

In mercy, King Providence, let him lie still!

He lied for a living; so he lived while he lied;

When he could not lie longer, he lied down and died.

From an Elkhart, Indiana, professor:

School is out, Teacher has gone home.

Found in Ruido, New Mexico:

Here lies John Yeast; Pardon me for not rising.

From the Wall Street Trinity Church cemetery:

Remember friends as you pass by,

As you are now, so once was I.

So, as I am you soon will be,

So prepare for death and follow me.

Someplace in a Maryland cemetery:
> Here lies the body of Jane Smith, wife of Thomas Smith,
> a marble cutter. This monument, erected as a tribute to her
> memory, may be duplicated for $250.

Ft. Wallace, Kansas:
> He tried to make 2 jacks beat a pair of aces.

Middletown, Maryland:
> I fought a good battle, but losted.

Connecticut:
> Here lies, cut down like unripe fruit,
> The wife of Deacon Amos Shute:
> She died drinking too much coffee,
> Anny dominy eighteen forty. (But what was her name?)

Holly, Michigan, cemetery:
> He did not reach 70 going like 60.

From the tombstone of a hypochondriac:
> I told you I was sick.

Today's Quote: *Once I wasn't, Then I was, Now I ain't, Again.* — Epitaph, Lee County, Mississippi

Today's Verse: For as in Adam all die, so in Christ all will be made alive. But each in his own turn: Christ, the firstfruits; then, when He comes, those who belong to Him (1 Cor. 15:22-23).

Day 15

Almost

Shortly after the Dallas Theological Seminary was founded in 1924, it almost didn't make it. It nearly went under . . . in fact, it came to the very point of bankruptcy and teetered on the edge. The creditors were planning to foreclose at noon on this particular day. Everything humanly possible had been tried. It was a gloomy day.

On this morning of doomsday, many of the faculty and board members met in the president's office with Dr. Chafer for prayer that God would somehow provide the miracle of finance. As it is the custom in Baptist circles, a prayer circle was formed and each man prayed in turn.

Among those present was Dr. Harry Ironside. When it was his turn to pray, he prayed in his characteristic-to-the-point manner: "Lord, we know that the cattle on a thousand hills are Thine. Please sell some of them and send us the money." When completed, the next person prayed and they continued on around this very concerned group of men.

While they were in their prayer meeting, a tall Texan with boots, jeans, and an open collared shirt walked into the business office and said to the receptionist, "I just sold two carloads of cattle in Fort Worth. I've been trying to make a business deal go through and it won't work and I've been compelled to give the money to the seminary and I don't know if you need it or not, but here's the check!"

That little secretary reached for the check, looked at the amount, and being well aware of the critical nature of the situation, immediately got up and headed in the direction of the prayer meeting. She timidly knocked, not wanting to disturb the prayers, but needing to get somebody's attention. She kept on tapping until finally, the president, Dr. Chafer went to the door. With great excitement she explained what had happened and handed him the check. Dr. Chafer took the check from her hand, looked at the amount only to see it was made out in exactly the amount for which they had been praying. He then glanced at the name on the check and recognized it as the cattleman from Forth Worth. He then turned around and returned to the prayer meeting which he interrupted in mid-prayer, turned to Dr. Harry Ironside, and almost shouted in his excitement, "Harry, God sold the cattle!"

Today, you may be hurting in a financial way. You may be questioning God and His provision. Hold on — God still cares and He still provides!

Today's Quote: *To pray is the greatest thing we can do, and to do it well, there must be calmness, time, and deliberation!* — E.M. Bounds

Today's Verse: And my God, with all His abundant wealth in Christ Jesus, will supply all your needs (Phil. 4:19;TEV).

The Pulpit Gaffe

Rev. Ron Prinzing, outstanding senior pastor of the First Family Church in Whittier, California, bemoans the verbal error that hurry creates. While serving as associate pastor of Bible Assembly in South Gate, California, he created an explosion of laughter.

The Sunday night service had already been long. The choir had unexpectedly sung two songs instead of one and then the church trio sang three songs. Between each song there were testimonies, as each of the women in the trio and members of the choir wanted to thank the Lord publicly for unique events in their lives. All this was good, but very time-consuming. As the last trio song was being sung, Rev. Prinzing looked at the clock and confirmed his uneasy feeling. It was already 8:45 and he had not yet preached.

A movement at the platform entrance door brought further anxiety. There stood his wife, Roselyn, and the head deacon, Frank Bunnell, violins in hand. They had prepared a special duet and were ready. Looking quickly in the direction of his wife, Prinzing shook his head no. She stared back and nodded her head yes! She pointed discretely to Frank Bunnell, indicating that he had really practiced for this and they must play their violins. When the trio finished, Prinzing moved swiftly to the pulpit. "Folks, we've had a wonderful Sunday night already. I do want to preach and will be careful to watch the time. He proceeded to give the announcements and then called the ushers forward to receive the evening offering, thinking to save time by having the violin duet play for the offertory. "Friends, thank you for your faithfulness," he said. "While you're giving tonight I'm going to call on Frank Bunnell to come and fiddle with my wife."

He did not catch this embarrassing slip. The violin duet was finished and Roselyn leaned over and whispered in her husband's ear what he had said. The congregation sat silent, but an explosion of laughter was on the verge of eruption. People were covering their faces. Ron Prinzing rose and returned to the pulpit. "You all know what I meant." There was a gush of laughter. "What I meant to say," he continued, "was that Brother Bunnell was going to play with my wife." Some people jumped up and headed for the door . . . their laughter could not be stalled. He should have left well enough alone. Everyone roared a second time![3]

This is a celebration of being human! Yes, we love God and our people love God, but the words come out wrong! "To the pure all things are pure." But that doesn't stop them from being hilarious! What do you say now? Simply, the benediction, "AMEN, folks, that's all!"

Today's Quote: *To mis-speak is human, but to really louse things up requires a computer.*

Today's Verse: For by your words you will be acquitted, and by your words you will be condemned (Matt. 12:37).

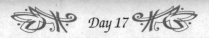

Are You Jesus?

A few years ago a group of salesmen went to a regional sales convention in Chicago. They had assured their wives that they would be home in plenty of time for Friday night's dinner.

Well, as such things go, one thing led to another, the sales manager went longer than anticipated and the meeting ran overtime. Their flights were scheduled to leave out of Chicago's O'Hare Airport and they had to race pell mell to the airport. With tickets in hand, they barged through the terminal to catch their flight back home. In their rush, with tickets and brief-cases, one of these salesmen inadvertently kicked over a table which held a display of baskets of apples. Apples flew everywhere. Without stopping or looking back they managed to reach the plane in time for their nearly missed boarding. All but one of these men.

He paused, took a deep breath, got in touch with his feelings, and experienced a twinge of compassion for the girl whose apple stand had been overturned. He told his buddies to go on without him, waved goodbye, told one of them to call his wife when they arrived at their home destination and explain his taking a later flight. Then he returned to the terminal where the apples were all over the terminal floor. He was glad he did. The 16-year-old girl was totally blind! She was softly crying, tears running down her cheeks in frustration, and at the same time helplessly groping for her spilled produce, as the crowd swirled about her, no one stopping, and no one to care for her plight.

This salesman knelt on the floor with her, gathered up the apples, put them into the baskets, and helped set the display up once more. As he did this, he noticed that many of them had become battered and bruised; these he set aside in another basket. When he had finished, he pulled out his wallet and said to the girl, "Here, please take this 20 for the damage we did. Are you okay?" She nodded through her tears. He continued on with, "I hope we didn't spoil your day too badly."

As the salesman started to walk away, the bewildered blind girl called out to him, "Mister. . . ."

He paused and turned to look back into those blind eyes.

She continued, "Are you Jesus?"[4]

He stopped in mid-stride. And he wondered. Then slowly he made his way to catch the later flight with that question burning and bouncing about in his soul: "Are you Jesus?"

What a question for anybody who touches people! ARE YOU JESUS?

Today's Quote: *The argument for the risen Christ is the living Christian.*
— Winifred Kirkland

Today's Verse: To them God has chosen to make known among the Gentiles the glorious riches of this mystery, which is Christ in you, the hope of glory (Col. 1:27).

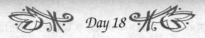

Day 18

The Sermon in Shoe Leather

One afternoon in 1953, reporters, officials, dignitaries, and the welcoming committee gathered at the Chicago railway station awaiting the arrival of the 1952 "Nobel Peace Prize" winner. There was naturally anticipation and excitement, even in Chicago. The train came to a halt and he stepped off the train — a giant of a man, just over six-feet-four-inches, erect in posture, with a thatch of bushy hair, a large moustache, and dressed simply in a cotton khaki suit and tie. The only thing missing was his trademark pith helmet.

Cameras flashed, city officials approached with outstretched hands. They presented him with a key to the city and began telling him how honored they were to meet him and welcomed him to the windy city. It was one of those formal kinds of occasions.

He expressed a polite thanks, then paused, as he was looking at something catching his attention over their heads. He looked at them and asked if he could be excused for a few moments. He then made his way through the waiting crowd with quick, firm strides until he reached the side of an elderly black lady who was struggling as she attempted to carry two rather large and heavy suitcases. No one had offered to help and everyone's attention was focused on the man who had just departed the train, now making his way to her side.

He nodded to the lady, picked up those two suitcases in his big hands, carried them to the open luggage compartment where the bus driver placed them on the rack, and with a smile escorted the lady to the waiting bus on which she apparently was making her way home following her train ride. Then he helped her aboard the bus, helped her find a seat, and wished her a safe journey and that someone would be at the other end to help her with her load.

Meanwhile, the crowd had tagged along behind him, observing this scene, and maybe all feeling a bit foolish and guilty for not having offered to help. He turned to them and said, "Sorry to have kept you waiting."

And the welcoming continued but with a different kind of atmosphere, almost in hushed tones of greeting. Almost as though something spiritual had taken place — it was sensed and not easily written about. The lesson was obvious.

The Nobel Peace Prize winner was the world-famous, missionary-doctor, Albert Schweitzer. A man who had spent his life helping the poorest of the poor in Africa. One of the members of the official reception committee turned to one of the *Chicago Times* reporters and said: "That's the first time I ever saw a sermon walking."

Today's Quote: *Is your Christianity ancient history or current events?* — Samuel M. Shoemaker

Today's Verse: And if anyone gives a cup of cold water to one of these little ones because he is my disciple, I tell you the truth, he will certainly not lose his reward (Matt. 10:42).

Hall of Famers Have Done It, Too

In the sports world, it's been easy to see the errors committed by some of the biggest names — even "Hall of Famers" have messed up. Here follows some of the biggest names in baseball, record holders all, but did you know about these other records they set? For example:

BABE RUTH — an absolutely awesome home run hitter with 714 in a career, a record which he held for 39 years. But he also held the strike-out record of 1,330 times until broken by another hall of famer.

TY COBB — fantastic competitor, batting champ, and the holder of most base steals in a season and a career until 1982. Cobb also held the record for being thrown out the most times attempting to steal in a season, 38 times in 1915.

CY YOUNG — terrific pitcher and still holds the most career victories, 511, in a lifetime. However, he also holds the record for most life-time losses, 313! He once posted a 13-win, 21-loss season.

HANK AARON — the home run slugger who bested Babe Ruth's career home run record with 755 homers. But Aaron holds the career mark for hitting into the most double plays, ever.

WALTER JOHNSON — one of the greatest pitchers, who, until recently bested, had posted the most strikeouts — 3,508. Johnson also holds the record for hitting the most batters — 204.

JIMMY FOXX — perhaps the greatest righthanded batter to ever play the game. He once hit 58 home runs in a season. And he holds the record for leading the league in strikeouts for the most consecutive seasons — seven!

ROBERTO CLEMENTE — famous Pittsburgh Pirate star struck out four times in one All-Star game — still a record.

SANDY KOUFAX — pitching sensation for the Dodgers, pitched four no-hitters in his career, but was a lousy batter. He still holds the record for striking out the most consecutive times at bat — 12!

REGGIE JACKSON — home run hitter for the Angels. On May 13, 1983, against the Twins, he became the first major leaguer to strike out 2,000 times. When asked what this kind of record meant to him, this slugging California Angel outfielder said, "It means I did nothing but miss the ball for four full seasons!"

So my pastor friend, take heart! In a few years after you've decided to hang it up, maybe history and people will be kind enough to remember our wins and forget the losses!

Today's Quote: *Managers are always learning, and mostly from our mistakes. That's why I keep a list of my mistakes at home for reference. I used to carry the list around in my pants pocket, but I finally had to stop. It gave me a limp.* — Earl Weaver, former baseball manager

Today's Verse: But we have this treasure in jars of clay to show that this all-surpassing power is from God and not from us (2 Cor. 4:7).

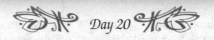

George Washington

George Washington, our first president, set a standard of quality for all Americans since his birth. Our beautiful country has seen many great men, heroes, excellent citizens, and people to be admired. But as we look back from our vantage point in history there has been no other, with the possible exception of Abraham Lincoln, who has been a living example of what we think great Americans should be.

He gave us a quality of leadership and living that was seen in the cherry tree incident of his childhood. He confessed his wrongdoing and went on to a special kind of maturity.

As I look back at history I see a man who was eager for life in a new nation, a nation that was forming and was still seeking an identity. The imprint of this man's life is still with us. Our nation's capital was named for him.

Here is a man who loved life as it was given to him. At the tender age of 20 he became the heir to Mt. Vernon and spent the next 20 years of his life in pursuit of the good life, in the social whirl, enjoying the power of his wealth.

We are told that on his fortieth birthday he went to a part of the vast lawn of Mt. Vernon overlooking the Potomac River and meditated, dreamed, and prayed about his future. It was at this moment that he gave himself to God and pledged his life to this new country. He started his public service in a humble position, that of adjutant in one of the five military districts of Virginia.

He left the comforts of home when he was called upon to serve his country. We next see him in the bitter winter of Valley Forge sharing the hardships with his men, providing them the standard. One of the most touching scenes is watching him kneel in the snow in the quiet of the woods, and there call upon God to aid his suffering, oppressed people.

Victory became his and then he was summoned once more to serve, as our first president. We see him walk away after giving two terms which could have become another Imperial kingdom, all without pay or any kind of remuneration. Thank you George Washington for setting a high standard for us!

Today's Quote: *It is impossible to rightly govern the world without God and the Bible!* — George Washington

Today's Verse: He has showed you, O man, what is good. And what does the Lord require of you? To act justly, and to love mercy and to walk humbly with your God. (Mic. 6:8). Washington's favorite verse of Scripture, which he quoted in a letter written on June 8, 1783, containing his prayer for the 13 states.

✝

The Gift of the Rabbi

There was a famous monastery which had fallen on hard times. Formerly its many buildings had been filled with young monks and its big church resounded with singing but now was nearly deserted. A handful of old monks shuffled through the cloisters and praised and prayed with heavy hearts. At the edge of the monastery woods, an old rabbi had built a little hut. He went there from time to time to pray and fast. No one ever spoke with him, but the word would be passed when he appeared, "The rabbi walks in the woods." And as long as he was there the monks felt sustained by his prayerful presence.

One day the abbot decided to visit the rabbi and to open his heart to him. As he approached the hut, the rabbi was standing in the doorway with outstretched arms in welcome. It was as though he had been waiting a long time. They embraced like long-lost brothers.

The rabbi motioned the abbot to enter. In the middle of the room was a plain wooden table with the Scripture open on it. They sat in the presence of the Book — then the rabbi began to cry, and as the abbot could not contain himself, he also began to cry. They filled the hut with the sound of their sobs.

After the tears had ceased and all was quiet, the rabbi said, "You and your brothers are serving God with heavy hearts. You have come to ask a teaching of me. I will give you this teaching but you can only repeat it once. After that, no one must say it aloud again."

Then the rabbi looked at the abbot and said, "The Messiah is among you." The abbot left without a word and without looking back.

The next morning he called his monks together and told them he had received a teaching from "the rabbi who walks in the woods" and this was never to be spoken again. Then he looked at each of his brothers and said, "The rabbi said that one of us is the messiah."

The monks were startled by this teaching but no one ever mentioned it again.

As time went by, the monks began to treat each other with a very special reverence. Visitors were deeply touched by their lives. People came from far and wide to be nourished by the prayer life of the monks, and young men asked about becoming part of this community. The rabbi no longer walked in the woods, but the monks who had taken his teaching to heart were still sustained by a prayerful presence.

Today's Quote: *There is in this world more hunger for love and appreciation than there is for bread, acclaim, or doctrinal purity.*

Today's Verse: Behold, how good and how pleasant it is For brethren to dwell together in unity! It is like the precious oil upon the head, Running down on the beard, The beard of Aaron, Running down on the edge of his garments. It is like the dew of Hermon . . . For there the Lord commanded the blessing . . . Life forever (Ps. 133:1-3;NKJV).

First Desire

John Jasper was a former slave, and following the Civil War, pastored the Sixth Mt. Zion Baptist Church in Richmond, Virginia. This was a great church.

He was preaching one Sunday morning about heaven and joys which will await us on the other side. He made an attempt to describe those beauties and the joys of heaven. His avid imagination and emotions were caught up and as he opened his mouth to speak he couldn't say a word. He tried several times and the great congregation sat in anticipation. He tried again but no sound. He was overcome with emotion.

Then the tears began to roll down his black cheeks. Still, as he would attempt to articulate, no sound would come out. Finally, he just shook his head and waved the crowd to the doors but they continued to sit. Then he walked to the side of the pulpit, with his hand on the door to his study and again waved the crowd toward home. Again no one moved.

Then, he moved to the pulpit and with great effort composed himself and leaned over it and said something like this: "Brothers and Sisters, when I think of the glory which shall be revealed in us, I can visualize that day when old John Jasper's last battle has been fought and the last burden has been borne. I can visualize that day when this tired servant of God shall lay down his burdens and walk up to the battlements of the City of God. I can almost hear the Mighty Angel on guard say 'John

Jasper, you want your shoes?' And I'se gonna say, 'Course I wants ma shoes, ma golden slippers to walk the gold-paved streets of the City of God, but not now.

"Then I can hear the Mighty Angel as he says, 'John Jasper, don't you want your robe?'

"I'se gonna say, 'Course I wants ma robe, that robe of linen clean and white which am the righteousness of the saints, but not now.'

"Then the Angel would say, 'John Jasper, you want your crown?'

"I shall say, 'Course, Mighty Angel. I wants all the reward that's comin' to me, this poor black servant of the Lamb, but not now.'

"Then the Angel would say, 'John Jasper, wouldn't you like to see Elijah, John the Beloved, and Paul?'

"I'll say, 'Course Mighty Angel. I wants to know and to shake hands and yes, I have loved ones over here, but not now. Fust, I wants to see Massa Jesus . . . I wants to see Him fust of all!' "[5]

Today's Quote: *Anybody who still thinks the sky is the limit has no imagination!* — Saturday Evening Post

Today's Verse: Then I saw a new heaven and a new earth, for the first heaven and the first earth had passed away, and there was no longer any sea. I saw the Holy City, the new Jerusalem (Rev. 21:1-2).

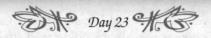 *Day 23*

Driven to the Edge

The enemy of our soul is wise in waging warfare — it's not so much in the big battles, but it's the constant hammering away in the little things! We are prepared for the major battles . . . but the drip, drip, erosion of the never ending attacks behind the scenes get to us. Here's a poem that seems to sum this struggle up. The author is unknown.

> I thought, if defeat came at all,
> It would be in a big, bold
> Definite joust
> With a cause or a name.
> And it came.
>
> I had not thought the daily skirmish
> With a few details, worthwhile;
> And so I turned my back upon them
> Year on year; until one day
> A million minutia blanketed together
> Rose up and overwhelmed me.

A pastor from Texas, who shall remain unnamed, was scheduled to speak at a minister's conference. He was running late because the alarm hadn't gone off. In his hurrying he cut himself while shaving — lots of blood. Then his shirt wasn't properly ironed from the dry-cleaners. And when he left the hotel, running to his car, he noticed a flat tire!

Really disgusted and harried by this time, quickly changing the tire, running back to his room to wash his hands, he finally got underway with a squeal of tires and a burst of speed. Racing through town he ran a stop sign. As fate or whatever would have it, a police squad was checking that intersection and he immediately heard the scream of a siren and saw the flashing of red lights!

Really agitated now, the minister jumped out of his car, nearly ran back to the patrol man, almost shouting, "Well, go ahead and give the ticket. Everything else has gone wrong today!" The policeman quietly got out of his car and walked to meet the minister saying quietly, "Sir, I used to have days like that before I became a Christian."

Well, needless to say, the quiet rebuke from this stranger did its work. The pastor apologized, chagrined, asked forgiveness, and went on his way . . . this time praying for strength and discipline to correct a faulty attitude.

Today's Quote: *Patience is the ability to keep your motor idling when you feel like stripping the gears.*

Today's Verse: Not only so, but we also rejoice in our sufferings, because we know that suffering produces perseverance; perseverance, character; and character, hope (Rom. 5:3-4).

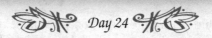

The Impact of a Leader

In September of 1862, the Civil War tilted decisively in favor of the South. The morale of the Northern army had dipped to its lowest point of the war. Large numbers of Union troops were in full retreat in Virginia. Northern leaders began to fear the worst. They could see no answer to turning the beaten, exhausted troops into an army again.

There was only one general with this kind of leadership. General George McClellan had trained these troops for combat and they loved him. The War Department or the president's Cabinet could not see the connection. Only President Abraham Lincoln recognized his remarkable leadership skills.

Lincoln, ignoring the protests of his advisors, reinstated McClellan in command. He told the general to ride to Virginia and give the troops something no other man on earth could give them: enthusiasm! strength! resolve! and hope! McClellan accepted the command. He mounted his huge horse and cantered down the dusty Virginia roads.

What happened next is impossible to explain. Northern leaders couldn't explain it. Union soldiers couldn't explain it. Even McClellan couldn't later explain it. As the general met the retreating Union columns, he waved his hat over his head and shouted encouragement. When these bedraggled, worn-out troops saw their beloved leader/teacher they took heart! They were stirred by the feeling that now things would be different!

Bruce Catton, the Civil War historian, describes this enthusiasm that grew when word spread up and down through the ranks that General George McClellan was back in command: "Down mile after mile of Virginia roads the stumbling columns came alive. Men threw their caps and knapsacks into the air, and yelled until they could yell no more . . . because they saw this dapper little rider outlined against the purple starlight.

"And this, in a way, was the turning point of the war. No one could ever quite explain how it happened. But whatever it was, it gave President Lincoln and the North exactly what it needed. And history was forever changed because of it."

This story out of our history dramatically illustrates the impact one leader can have on the human being! General George McClellan inspired these burned-out troops to take another grip on life. That's why leaders are leaders! That's the challenge of the pastor/leader who points to the ultimate leader — Jesus Christ!

Today's Quote: *No pastor can lead who does not love the people he/she may be called upon to lead.*

Today's Verse: For you yourselves know how you ought to follow our example. We were not idle when we were with you. . . . We did this, not because we do not have the right to such help, but in order to make ourselves a model for you to follow (2 Thess. 3:7, 9).

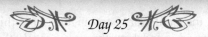

The Fourth Wise Man

The Gospels do not tell us how many wise men, or magi, journeyed to Bethlehem following the star. Popular tradition holds that there were three — Caspar, Melchior, and Balthasar. But there is also a tradition of a fourth wise man, named Artaban.

As Artaban prepared to set out and follow the star, he took with him a sapphire, a ruby, and a pearl of great price as gifts to the newborn King, whenever He was to be found.

On his way to join the other wise men, Artaban stopped to care for a sick traveler. If stayed to help, however, he would miss the rendezvous with his friends. He stayed, and the delay was just enough to make him late for the departure of the caravan. Now Artaban was alone, and he needed transportation and supplies to cross the desert. So he sold the sapphire to purchase camels and supplies. He was saddened because the King would never have this precious gem.

Artaban journeyed onward and reached Bethlehem, but again he was too late. There were soldiers everywhere to carry out Herod's command that the male children should be slain. Artaban, therefore, took out the brilliant ruby to bribe the captain and save the children in the village in which he was staying. Children were saved, mothers rejoiced; but the ruby, also, would not reach the King.

For 33 years Artaban searched in vain and finally found his way to

Jerusalem on the day several crucifixions were to take place. Artaban hurried towards Calvary in order to bribe the roman guard with the precious pearl and save the man called Jesus. Something told him that this was the King of kings for whom he had been searching all his life.

Just then, a young woman was being dragged along the street toward the slave market, called out to Artaban, pleading for help. With only a slight hesitation, he gave the last jewel, the pearl of great price, for her ransom. Now Artaban had none of the precious gems he was going to present to the King.

Reaching the place where the crucifixions were to occur he was heartbroken when he saw that he could do nothing to help Jesus. But then something remarkable happened. Jesus looked over toward Artaban and said to him: "Don't be brokenhearted, Artaban. You've been helping Me all your life. When I was hungry, you gave Me food, when I was thirsty, you gave Me drink, when I was naked, you clothed Me, when I was a stranger, you took Me in."

Some say Artaban never found Christ. Others say he was the wisest of the wise men.[6]

Today's Quote: *He is no fool who gives what he cannot keep, to gain what he cannot lose.* — Jim Elliot, missionary martyr

Today's Verse: The King will reply, "I tell you the truth, whatever you did for one of the least of these brothers of mine, you did for Me" (Matt. 25:40).

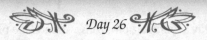

Keeper of the Springs

There was a quiet forest dweller who lived high above an Austrian village along the eastern slope of the Alps. The old gentleman had been hired many years ago by an earlier town council to clear away the debris of leaves and branches from the pristine springs up in the mountain ravines. These springs fed the pool from which the town gathered its water supply.

With consistency, the old man patrolled the surrounding hills, removed dead leaves and branches, and cleared away the dirt, dead animals, and silt that otherwise would clog and contaminate the fresh supply of water. In time, the village prospered and became a popular vacation spot for tourists. The mill wheels ran day and night, farmlands were irrigated, the water was unpolluted, the village healthy, and it was picture-postcard beautiful.

Years passed. At one town council meeting to review the budget, one member noticed the salary figure paid to the obscure "keeper-of-the-springs." The treasurer questioned the expense and asked, "Who is this old man? Who hired him? Is he productive?" The treasurer paused, then went on, "For all we know, this stranger up in the hills might be dead. He isn't needed any longer." So by a unanimous voice vote the council did away with the old man's services.

For several weeks nothing happened . . . all seemed to continue as it had been. Then came autumn, leaves were dropping, small branches snapped off, silt began to fall into the springs, and the flow began to slow. One householder noticed a slight yellowish-brown tint in the water. In a few days the gathering pool showed more dark color. In another week, a slime began covering some sections of the canal banks . . . then an odor was detected. The mill wheels ground to a halt, tourists disappeared, children began to get sick.

Quickly, the embarrassed town council called a special meeting. They realized their error. They voted to re-hire the old keeper of the springs and within several weeks the sparkling river of life cleared up . . . mill wheels turned again, tourists came back, children stopped being sick, and a renewed life returned to this Alpine village!

And what was the name of the old "Keeper-of-the-Springs"? Well, according to this story which has been told and retold in many versions, if you were to research the town records you will find his name possibly recorded as: Integrity, love, character, sound doctrine, prayer, Jesus, Joshua, perseverance, solid homes — well, you get the idea. And now that you know, you can put most anything foundational in as the keeper of your springs. We, personally, as well as the people we lead all are in need of the KEEPER OF THE SPRINGS!

Today's Quote: *For every human problem, there is a solution that is simple, neat . . . and wrong!* — H. L. Mencken

Today's Verse: Above all else, guard your heart, for it is the wellspring of life (Prov. 4:23).

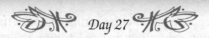

Does It Represent You?

In a particular church they had experienced such growth it demanded that they enlarge their facilities. It represented quite a step of faith. After much planning, praying, and working together, they decided on a new church building. It would be adequate for their expanded ministry. It was an exciting moment as together they came to the moment to begin raising funds for this multi-million dollar project.

The pastor and church board made their projections, along with their appeal to the congregation to share in this need by sacrificial giving. Everyone was challenged to be part of this expansion project.

After the service was over a lady came to the pastor personally and handed him a check for $50, asking at the same time if her gift was satisfactory. The pastor immediately replied, "If it represents you." There was a moment or two of soul-searching and she asked to have the check returned to her. She left with it.

A day or two later she returned to make an appointment to see the pastor. This time she handed the pastor her check for $5,000 and again asked the same question, "Is my gift satisfactory?"

The pastor gave the same answer as before, "If it represents you." As before, the truth seemed to be sinking deep into her mind. After some moments of quiet hesitation she took back the check and left. Now the pastor was beginning to get a bit worried. Perhaps he had been too bold and had offended her. He also wondered if she would ever return.

About two weeks later there was a phone call at the church office asking for another appointment with the pastor. It was the same woman. As before, she came with a check in hand and a big smile on her face. This time the check was for $50,000. As she placed it in the pastor's hand she said, "After earnest, prayerful thought, I have come to the conclusion that this gift does represent me, and I am most happy to give it to the church for our new project."

Money and giving are always touchy subjects to many people. Why? Do we have guilt in this area of our Christian living? Are we too selfish about the material things in our living? Giving and living are two things that go together in the Christian lifestyle. The Bible talks about sacrificial giving as well as cheerful giving. Just another question: Will your giving this week really represent you?

Today's Quote: *Give, not from the top of your purse, but from the bottom of your heart!* — David McConaughy

Today's Verse: On every Lord's Day each of you should put aside something from what you have earned during the week, and use it for this offering. The amount depends on how much the Lord has helped you earn (1 Cor. 16:2;LB).

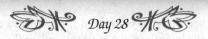

Acres of Diamonds

This classic story, "Acres of Diamonds" was told by Rev. Russell Conwell more than 5,000 times! The proceeds from this provided the funds to found Temple University. The story:

Is about a wealthy farmer who was probably one of the richest men in Africa. Hafid owned a large farm with fertile soil, herds of camels and goats, orchards of dates and figs. One day a wandering holy man visited his farm and mentioned that huge fortunes were being made discovering and mining diamonds — fortunes greater than even Hafid's.

This news captured Hafid's attention. He inquired of the holy man what diamonds were and where they could be found. The holy man said he wasn't sure of all the details but he had heard that diamonds were usually found in the white sands of rivers that flowed out from valleys formed by V-shaped mountains.

Hafid, eager to increase his fortune, sold his farm, herds, and orchards. He placed his family in the care of someone else and set out to find his fortune. Hafid's travels took him all over Africa. Finally, in deep despair he threw himself off a mountain and died a frustrated, broken, poor man.

The farmer that bought his farm was watering his camels one day and noticed a pretty rock in the river, because it sparkled. He took it home and put it on a shelf where the sun would strike it and splash rainbows of color across the room.

The same wandering holy man came back to this same farm. He was immediately startled by the rainbow of light from the rock. Had Hafid returned? Well, no he hadn't, and he was no longer the owner of this farm.

Then taking the rock from the shelf, the holy man became animated. "That's a diamond!" he excitedly told the farmer. "Where did you find it?" The farmer, somewhat confused in the flurry of excitement explained that it came from down by the river.

"Show me," insisted the holy man.

The two of them went out to the river, which flowed out from a valley formed by a V-shaped mountain. And there, in the white sands, they found a larger diamond, then another, and many more diamonds, large and small.

Actually the land, which Hafid sold to pursue his fortune elsewhere, turned out to be acres and acres of diamonds. In fact, it became the Kimberly, the richest diamond mine in all of South Africa![7]

Today's Quote: *The grass always looks greener on the other side of the fence — but remember that it, too, must be mowed, watered, fertilized, and weeded.*

Today's Verse: The worries of this life, the deceitfulness of wealth and the desires for other things come in and choke the word, making it unfruitful (Mark 4:19).

Pillars

Famed English architect Sir Christopher Wren designed a large dome for a church that was so unique he became the object of much criticism among his colleagues. During the construction of this dome they created so much fuss that the authorities demanded Wren add two huge supporting pillars to keep the dome from collapsing. Wren bitterly objected, insisting on the strength of his structure and the wisdom of his new architectural innovation. Besides, it would ruin the beauty and asthetics of the church. But the opposition was well-organized and powerful. The two pillars were added to the design over Wren's objections.

Fifty years passed since the construction of the controversial dome. It was now time to repaint the interior of the church, as well as the dome.

When the painters had erected their scaffolding to begin the painting they made the startling discovery that the two added pillars did not even touch the dome! They were short by two feet!

Sir Christopher Wren had such confidence in his work that he made sure the offending pillars were freestanding. The authorities, during his lifetime, came to make their inspection from the floor, saw the pillars, and assumed they reached the roof. They now felt secure, even though the pillars were freestanding and didn't support anything! Wren went to his grave with his little secret well-kept. I believe he may have had the last laugh at their expense. What a great little story!

Man has built many pillars to support his little world and to keep things from falling in on him. Often they seem strong and are able to stand the stress of time. But often they are just as useless as architect Wren's false columns.

Some have constructed pillars of religion, beautiful in structure and they seem strong enough. But religion is totally meaningless without the person of Jesus. Pillars of religion are freestanding without Christ and have no hold on eternity.

Others have erected pillars of intellectualism, money, pleasure, or philosophy. Lest we despair, there is a structure that is ample for the ultimate crisis of life. As Wren had confidence in his architectural creation, so can you have confidence in the structure God builds!

Today's Quote: *Christ is not valued at all unless He is valued above all!* — Augustine

Today's Verse: I am sending Christ to be the carefully chosen, precious Cornerstone of my church, and I will never disappoint those who trust in him (1 Pet. 2:6;LB).

More Than One Way

Just before the morning service was about to begin on a beautiful fall day at Saint Bartholomew's Episcopalian Church on Fifth Avenue in New York City, a man wearing a very large hat was discovered to be sitting in the very front row! An usher hurried from the back, moved to this pew, leaned in toward the man with the large hat and discreetly asked him to please remove his hat. The man replied, "No, thank you."

The usher almost ran to the usher station in the back of the church and asked for the head usher. Who in turn, after being told about the situation, made his way to the front and made the same request of the man with the large hat and received the exact same answer.

About that time the president of the women of the parish arrived at the main entrance to overhear the conversation of the head usher in regards to the rude man with the large hat in the front row. She offered to be of assistance. She made her way to the front pew, leaned in and as graciously as she could, she asked him to please remove his hat. She had the same dismal response, "No!"

Finally, only two minutes remained before the opening hymn and the senior warden of the parish was summoned. He had the solution! He carefully tiptoed up beside the man and reached out to grab the hat, but the man saw him and his tactic in time, and was able to nimbly dodge and the hat remained firmly in place. There was no more time for any other kind of an attempt.

As the opening hymn began and the choir made their procession into the church, the man stood with the rest of the congregation, removed his hat and did not put it on again, until the service was concluded.

At the conclusion of the service, the four frustrated people waited for the man at the rear of the church. The senior warden approached him and said, "Sir, about the hat. Perhaps you don't understand, but in the Episcopal Church men do not wear hats at worship."

The man replied, "Oh, but I do understand. I've been an Episcopalian all my life. As a matter of fact, I've been coming to this church regularly for the past two years and I've never met a soul. But this morning I've met an usher, the head usher, the president of the church women, and the senior warden, thank you all."

Ouch! Another reminder to do what we know we should do in church!

Today's Quote: *Few things are harder to put up with than the annoyance of a good example!* — Mark Twain

Today's Verse: Even my close friend, whom I trusted, he who shared my bread, has lifted up his heel against me (Ps. 41:9).

NOTES

1. William Goodin (Lima, OH: CSS Publishing Co., 1990).
2. Leslie R. Smith.
3. Sam Sasser, *Let Us Continue to Hold Sister Smith's Leg Up in Prayer!* (Shippensburg, PA: Treasure House, 1993), page 39.
4. Brian Cavanaugh, quoting Brennan Manning, *More Sower's Seeds* (Mahwah, NJ: Paulist Press, 1992).
5. G. Beauchamp Vick.
6. Henry Van Dyke.
7. Russell Conwell.

Moments to Give series

Moments for Christmas

Moments for Each Other

Moments for Fathers

Moments for Friends

Moments for Graduates

Moments for Grandparents

Moments for Mothers

Moments for Pastors

Moments for Sisters

Moments for Teachers

Moments for Teens

Moments with Angels

Available at bookstores nationwide or write
New Leaf Press, P.O. Box 726, Green Forest, AR 72638